Lettuce LAUGH

600 CORNY JOKES About Food

·NATASHA WING·

STERLING CHILDREN'S BOOKS
New York

To my husband, Dan, who
always makes me laugh

STERLING CHILDREN'S BOOKS
New York

An Imprint of Sterling Publishing Co., Inc.
1166 Avenue of the Americas
New York, NY 10036

ISBN 978-1-4549-3125-6

Distributed in Canada by Sterling Publishing Co., Inc.
c/o Canadian Manda Group, 664 Annette Street
Toronto, Ontario M6S 2C8, Canada
Distributed in the United Kingdom by GMC Distribution Services
Castle Place, 166 High Street, Lewes, East Sussex BN7 1XU, England
Distributed in Australia by NewSouth Books
45 Beach Street, Coogee, NSW 2034, Australia

For information about custom editions, special sales, and premium and
corporate purchases, please contact Sterling Special Sales at 800-805-5489
or specialsales@sterlingpublishing.com.

Manufactured in Canada

Lot #:
2 4 6 8 10 9 7 5 3 1
08/18

sterlingpublishing.com

Cover design by Elizabeth Mihaltse Lindy
Cover art components by Shutterstock.com

Contents

Salad Sillies 5

Veggie Varieties 7

Berry Funny Fruit 15

Animal Crackers 22

Cultural Cut-ups 26

Brain Freezers 32

Fishy Funnies 35

Put a Fork In It 39

Monstrous Mash-ups 43

Score with Sports Jokes 49

Meat Mania 51

Breakfast Crack-ups 58

Bread Winners 64

Bean Busters & Nutty Jokes 67

Junk Food Funnies 71

Baked Goodies 77

Top This! 81

Thirst Quenchers 83

A Potluck of Puns 85

Sweet & Sour 91

About the Author 96

SALAD SILLIES

What's the coldest vegetable?

Iceberg lettuce.

Why can you trust lettuce to keep secrets?

Because they keep them under wraps.

What's a salad's favorite game?

Toss.

What test did the salad pass?

The bar exam.

What did the justice of the peace say when the arugula and the romaine tied the knot?

"Lettuce join these two in marriage."

Knock, knock!

Who's there?

Lettuce.

Lettuce who?

Lettuce in, it's cold out here!

What did the bug say when it reached the top of the salad?

"This is just the tip of the iceberg lettuce!"

REFEREE FLIPPING A COIN: Heads or tails?
LETTUCE: Heads!

How do you weigh a salad?

In crou-tons.

Why was the salad not in the bar?

It was tossed out.

Why did the lettuce and cauliflower make good partners?

Two heads are better than one.

Why are leprechauns so healthy?

They eat a lot of greens.

Where do vegetables grow best?

Greenland.

CUCUMBER TO SALAD: Hurry up or we'll be late to the party.
SALAD: Just a minute! I'm dressing.

Knock, knock.
    Who's there?
Turnip.
    Turnip who?
Turnip the music and lettuce dance!

VEGGIE VARIETIES

What do vegetables say when they are minding their manners?
    "Peas" and "thank you."

Knock, knock.
    Who's there?
Olive.
    Olive who?
Olive next door. Want to play?

Why was the mushroom invited to every party?
    He was a fun-gi!

So why did that make the broccoli so angry?
    He was steaming mad that he wasn't invited.

Why did the cucumber stop working on its invention?

It didn't relish the idea.

What's the most expensive vegetable?

A golden beet.

Which vegetable never runs out of fuel?

Aspara-gas.

Knock, knock.

Who's there?

Turnip.

Turnip who?

Turnip the oven to 400°!

What's the baby pea's favorite game?

Pea-kaboo.

What did the vegan chef say about his latest creation?

"Make no bones about it, vegetable soup is delicious!"

HA HA HA HA HA

Overheard in the Produce Section

"Did you hear that Patty aced the spelling bee?"

"She's as cool as a cucumber."

Can you say this five times fast?

"A rash of radish rashes."

Why was the cabbage envied by all the other students?

Because it was at the head of its class.

Why did the cabbage run for president?

Because it wanted to be head of state.

Why was the potato burnt?

Because it was twice baked.

What do you get when you cross a cucumber with a feather?

A pickled tickler.

HA HA HA HA HA HA HA HA

Why are *chili* peppers so hot?

What was the celery in jail for?
Stalking!

How do peas listen to music?
On their iPods.

Why did the pod leave the salad bar?
It had to pea!

What do you call a pea that falls off your plate?
An escape-pea.

How do you make split-pea soup?
Cut the pea in half.

How do you make split-pea soup with ham?
Find a pig that cooks.

What do peas turn into after a fight?

Black-eyed peas.

Knock, knock.

Who's there?

Gourd.

Gourd who?

Gourd right ahead.

What did the leprechaun serve for St. Patrick's Day dinner?

A pot of Yukon gold potatoes.

What kind of vegetable is stored in a basement?

Cellar-y.

What do you get when you cross a pair of glasses and a pea?

An eye-pod.

Why was the carrot good at math?

Because it could do square roots.

Why won't the baby vegetable wear a diaper?

Because the diaper leeks.

HA HA HA HA HA HA HA HA

How do you fix a hole in a pumpkin?

With a pumpkin patch.

What vegetable do you eat when you're thirsty?

Watercress.

Which fall vegetable is most cautious?

A better-not squash.

What do you get when you cross a female pop singer with asparagus?

Britney Spears.

What happens when you put a 5-cent coin in a pumpkin?

You get pumpernickel.

What vegetable do you keep in your socks?

Pota-*toes.*

Which potato is the nicest, kindest potato of them all?

The sweet potato.

HA HA HA

What did the butter say to the hot potato?

"You make me melt."

What do you call an old potato dish?

Potato au rotten.

Why did the gardener feel like she was being watched?

Because the potatoes have eyes.

Why was the vegetable so affordable?

Because it was dirt cheap.

Why was the onion so hot?

It was wearing too many layers.

Why was the song so popular?

It had a good beet.

Why does corn love listening to Mozart?

It's music to its ears.

What do you get when you cross a pony and a root vegetable?

Horseradish.

HA HA HA HA HA HA HA HA

What do you call a zucchini after an elephant sits on it?

Squash!

What kind of jewelry did the scuba diver give the cook?

A pearl onion necklace.

Knock, knock.

Who's there?

Artichoke.

Artichoke who?

Artichoked on a piece of meat!

Why did the artichoke go to the doctor?

It had heart burn.

Why are corn good listeners?

Because they're all ears.

What does the baby corn call its father?

Pop corn!

Why were the two pieces of fruit so in love?

They made a good pear.

What did the leader of the fruit band say before they started playing?

"What kiwi in?"

How did the watermelon start up a business?

With seed money.

Did you hear about the banana that had a terrible day at the beach?

It was in the sun too long and started to peel.

Which fruit never goes anywhere alone?

A pear.

Where do watermelons put their money?

In seed banks.

HA HA HA

Why did it take so long for the raspberries to drive home?

They were in a traffic jam.

Best Self-help Books for Peaches

How to Overcome Pit-falls

How to Smoothie Out Your Relationships

25 A-peel-ing Places to Travel

*When Things Aren't Peachy:
How to Grow Fruitful Connections*

How to Get Out of a Jam

What to Do When Your Life Is the Pits

Knock, knock.

Who's there?

Figs.

Figs who?

Figs a side dish and bring it to the potluck!

HA

What kind of countertop does a cook have?

Pome-granite.

What do you call statues of fruit?

Fig-urines.

Knock, knock.
    Who's there?
Rhubarb?
    Rhubarb who?
No, I'm her sister.

Where did the vineyard workers hear all their gossip?
    Through the grape vine.

How many pits should a pitter spit, if a pitter could spit pits?

Why didn't the monkey eat the banana?
    It didn't look a-peel-ing.

Why was the grape a hit on the dance floor?
    Because it loved raisin' the roof!

Can you say this five times fast?

"Fifty-five fun fruit frappe flavors."

HA HA HA

Why was the peach kicked out of presidential office?

It was impeached!

Which city do cherries like best?

Pittsburgh.

What kind of bed would fruit prefer to sleep on?

Apri-cot!

What's the most misleading fruit name?

Pineapples, because they grow on neither pine nor apple trees.

Why did the banana go to the doctor?

It wasn't peeling well.

What do you call a fruit that writes plays?

Shakespear.

What did the Bartlett pears become when they had a baby?

Pearants!

What fruit is as hard as a rock?

Pome-granite!

What do you call fruit traveling by airplane?

Fruit flies!

How do you mix fruits and vegetables?

With a blender.

What do you call a negative melon?

A *can't*-eloupe.

How is a calendar like bacon wraps?

It's full of dates!

Why did the peaches look so young?

They were well preserved.

Can you say this five times fast?

"Reach beneath each peach."

What do you call shoes made out of banana peels?

Slippers!

How did the grocery man sell his fruit?

In pears.

Knock, knock!

Berry.

Berry who?

Berry sorry to bother you, but I forgot my key.

What do you get when you cross a blueberry and a yellow berry?

A green berry.

Which is the saddest berry?

The blueberry.

Which berry often gets bogged down?

The cranberry.

What do you call a gold miner who crushes berries?

A sluicer juicer.

Knock, knock.

Who's there?

Marion.

Marion who?

Marionberry and you're invited to the wedding.

HA HA HA HA HA HA HA HA

What kind of berries are hard to swallow?

Chokeberries.

Which berry makes an awful noise?

Rasp-berry.

Which berry can sing?

Berry Manilow!

Why was *The Berry Patch* newspaper canceled?

It couldn't stay currant.

What kind of Thanksgiving sauce should you avoid spreading on turkey legs?

Cramp-berry!

Knock, knock.

(...)

KNOCK, KNOCK.

Who's there?

Berry.

Berry who?

Berry rude of you not to answer on the first knock.

HA HA HA

ANIMAL CRACKERS

Why was the monkey a big eater?

Because he had a good ape-etite.

What do you call a dog that loves lots of pasta?

An oodle noodle poodle.

Knock, knock.

Who's there?

Wok.

Wok who?

Wok your dog—he's been barking for an hour!

What was Lassie's favorite vegetable?

Collie-flower.

What dessert does a cat like?

Chocolate mouse.

What does a dentist call a bear without teeth?

A gummy bear!

HA HA HA HA HA HA HA HA

What did the bunny give to his girlfriend?

A one-carrot ring.

How do cats beat eggs?

With their whiskers.

What do you call a female deer smothered in guacamole?

Avoca-doe!

What did Little Miss Muffet get when she crossed cottage cheese and a horse?

Curds and neigh!

Where do ranchers raise beef?

Salt Lick City.

Why do pigs make great partners?

They bring home the bacon.

What do you call a brown cow with no legs?

Ground beef!

What do you call a twitchy cow?

Beef jerky.

What do you call a pig that steals?
    A hamburglar.

What do you call a slow pig?
    Bacon.

What kind of cake did the rabbit want for its birthday?
    Carrot!

What's the frog's favorite fast food?
    French flies.

How do you make monkey bread rise?
    With a banana!

Why did the donkey put hot sauce on his food?
    To give it some kick.

Why was the horse so frisky?
    He was sowing his oats.

What kind of bread goofs off?
    Monkey bread.

PUPPY: What's for dinner?
DOG: Catfish.

What do you get when you add an *s* to *mouse*?

Mousse.

What kind of dessert do cats like?

Mice pudding.

Can you say this five times fast?

"Messy mouse mooches mousse."

How do you open a honey jar?

With bear claws!

What's the opposite of a hot dog?

A cold cat.

How do you make a hot dog?

Put a dog out in the sun.

What do gorillas sleep on?

Ape-ri-cots!

Where do you send a bad sled dog?

To his *mush*room.

What side dish do cats like?

Mice and beans.

What's a pig's favorite dessert?

Mud pie!

CULTURAL CUT-UPS

Why was the pizza man so rich?

He was rolling in dough!

How do you fix a pizza slice?

With tomato paste.

What instant pasta does the pope eat?

Roman noodles.

What happens when you eat too much tomato sauce?

Paste makes waist.

What do you call a stolen frozen pizza?

Take and bake.

BOY: Are you going to eat your pizza?

GIRL: No.

TEENAGER: Hey! Who ate my pizza?

BOY TO GIRL: I thought you said you weren't going to eat your pizza?

GIRL: It's not my pizza.

What does the Italian chef fall asleep on?

Pasta pillows.

What did the spaghetti say to the macaroni when they parted ways?

"Pasta la vista!"

Best Self-help Books for Pizzas

Math Made Simple with Pizza Pie Charts
A Slice of Life
Rolling in Dough
How to Live Like the Upper Crust
Think Outside the Box

HA HA HA HA HA
HA HA HA HA HA

How much does pasta cost?

One penne.

How do you ask to pass a dish at a spaghetti dinner party?

"*Pasta* sauce, please."

What do you call a phony noodle?

An impasta!

What did the yeast say to the matzo?

"I can't get a rise out of you!"

What do you call a lucky *Star Wars* character?

Fortune Wookiee.

What kind of rice can tell time?

Minute rice.

What's the baby's favorite children's book?

The Ugly Dumpling.

What do Chinese chickens eat?

"Bawk" Choy.

HA HA HA HA HA

What is a lumberjack's favorite Asian dish?

Chop Suey.

What game show is always on TV at the Chinese restaurant?

Wheel of Fortune Cookie.

Fortune Cookie Fortunes

A wise person would have ordered a real dessert.

That's the way the cookie crumbles!

If you take advice from a cookie, then your life will be half-baked.

Eat this cookie before eating your words.

Can you say this five times fast?

"One wonton with Juan."

CUSTOMER: Is this chili?

WAITRESS: No, it's hot.

HA HA HA HA HA

What do you get when you cross poultry with a small burrowing animal?

Chicken mole.

What arcade game do you play with an avocado?

Guac-A-Mole.

What do you get when you layer refried beans, shredded cheese, salsa, chopped lettuce, and sour cream on toasted bread?

A toast-ada!

What do you get when you spit out hot peppers?

Pepper spray!

Sign in a Mexican Restaurant

IN QUESO EMERGENCY, EXIT HERE!

What do you make peculiar guacamole with?

Odd-vocadoes.

HA HA HA

What kind of Mexican food does a donkey like?
Burro-ito!

What do you chant at Mexican operas?
Bravocado!

What do you get when you cross beef and tortillas?
Cow chips.

WEATHERMAN: It's chili today but will be hot tamale.

What is a nacho's favorite type of dance?
The salsa.

What do you call a small Mexican dog that eats through all his toys?
Chew-huahua.

Why was the boy's Mexican food served cold?
He ordered a *brrrrito!*

HA HA HA HA HA HA

BRAIN FREEZERS

What did the policeman say to the melting popsicle?

"Freeze!"

How do you make ice cream?

Shout "BOO!"

What's black and white and blue all over?

A panda eating a blueberry Icee.

What's the best day to buy ice cream?

Sundae!

Why do ice cream cones make good reporters?

Because they always get the scoop.

Why did the popsicle fail the taste test?

It was a bomb pop.

Why are bomb pops so popular?

Because they're a blast to eat!

Why was the ice cream left alone?
Because the banana split.

Where do polar bears shop for groceries?
In the frozen food section.

How do polar bears keep their food fresh?
Seal wrap.

What do polar bears eat as a side dish?
Iceberg lettuce.

What country is really good at keeping food cold?
Iceland.

Why did the football team put their opponent's kicker in the freezer?
They wanted to ice him.

Where do ice cream makers get their training?
Sundae school.

HA HA HA HA HA

Can you say this five times fast?

"Dipping dots are dripping lots."

Where does a snowman put his ice cream?

In a snow cone.

What kind of food does a snowman eat?

Frozen!

What's a snowman's favorite cookie?

A snowball!

What does a polar bear store his fish in?

An Arctic cooler.

What do you get when you put a vampire in the freezer?

Frostbite!

What do you get when you cross a shellfish and a baked good?

A crab cake!

How many courses does an octopus eat?

Eight!

Which crustacean loves movies?

Popcorn shrimp.

Why won't the clam share?

It's shellfish.

What does the scuba diver say when he can't find any shellfish?

A-balone!

HA HA HA

"How many shellfish should a sea lion sell, if a sea lion could sell shellfish?"

What did the lobster say when he won the lottery?

"Pinch me!"

Why did the lobster turn red?

He was boiling mad.

Overheard at a Fish Fry

"Did you know that Bobby fibbed about the size of the trout he caught?"

"I knew something smelled fishy."

What did the grandma lobster say to the baby lobster?

"Oh, you're so cute, I just want to pinch you!"

HA HA HA HA HA

What's a fish's scariest day of the week?

Fry-day.

Can you say this five times fast?

"Five fussy fishies fish for food while Wiley's wishing wishes."

Why didn't the fish eat the worm?

It was filled to the gills.

What do you call tiny crustaceans with a lot of courage?

Shrimp with grits.

How does a lobster like his chowder?

With a pinch of salt.

How is lobster served in New England?

As a Maine course.

HA HA HA HA HA

Overheard at a Lobster Bake

"Did you hear that Julie might get
cut from the school play?"

"She butter get her act together."

What's the leprechaun's favorite fish dish?

Rainbow trout.

How did the boy get strong?

He ate mussel soup.

Can you say this five times fast?

"Shelly's elf is selfishly selling shellfish."

PUT A FORK IN IT

What did the justice of the peace say when he married the skillet and the cutlery?

"I now pronounce you pan and knife."

Why did the hiker stop to eat?

There was a fork in the trail.

Why won't the cheese wear underwear?

It doesn't want to get a wedgie.

What did the kettle say to the boiling pot?

"Put a lid on it."

What kitchen tool do cats use?

A whisker!

Why did the miner sauté his yellow beets?

He was panning for gold.

Why did the spoon get arrested?

It was a cereal killer.

What did the spoon say to the plate?

"You can dish it out, but you can't take it!"

What do you get when you cross a fork and a knife?

Poked!

What did the worried psychiatrist ask the cook?

Do garlic presses ever get de-pressed?

Why was the pan so admired by its friends?

It always had a handle on the situation.

Why does the boy have metal fillings?

He was born with a silver spoon in his mouth.

What is a cook's favorite Christmas greeting?

"We whisk you a Merry Christmas!"

What does a fork have in common with a fish?

Both can be tuned.

At the end of a cooking class, what does a chef use to correct his students' tests?

A grater!

Knock, knock.
Who's there?
Gouda.
Gouda who?
Gouda to meet you!

Why did the Cheeses get a divorce?
There was too big of a wedge between them.

How do you eat cheese?
Any way you slice it.

What did the cheddar say to the photographer?
"Cheese!"

Which princess ended up on a pizza instead of in a palace?
Mozza-rella.

Why does the Swiss cheese live in a church?
Because it is so hole-y.

How did the dairyman tie his boots?
With string cheese.

HA HA HA HA HA

What's the mouse's favorite game show?

Wheel of Cheese.

What did the Vermont cheddar say to the white cheddar?

"My, you've aged!"

Knock, knock.

Who's there?

Fondue.

Fondue who?

Fondue hiding behind the door!

What cheese is named after a kind of dwelling?

Cottage cheese.

MONSTROUS MASH-UPS

What happens when you feed Frankenstein cheese?

He turns into a muenster!

What do you get when you cross a cupcake with a monster?

Crumbs.

What do you call Bigfoot's favorite pasta?

Spa-yeti.

What did Bigfoot say to the giant, hairy pumpkin?

"I don't believe in sa-squashes."

What do you call a ghost that haunts an oven?

A boo-berry turnover!

What did the alien say to the bottle of soda?

"Take me to your liter."

What's a ghoul's favorite stew?

Ghoulash!

GHOST: Good moaning!

WAITRESS: Good morning. What would you like for breakfast?

GHOST: A boo-berry muffin, please, with a glass of evaporated milk.

Why didn't the vampires want to go to the fancy restaurant?

They knew there'd be a lot of stakes there. (Garlic, too!)

What monsters bring to a Halloween potluck

Vampires—blood sausages
Frankenstein—frankenbeans
Witches—sandwitches
Skeletons—dead bread (Pan de Muerto)
Zombies—undead bread
Ghosts—ice scream

HA HA HA HA HA
HA HA HA HA HA

What kind of dessert do swamp monsters eat?

Marsh-mallows!

What do you get when you cross a turkey and a monster?

A gobbling goblin.

What did the vampire say to the citrus grower?

"I want to suck your blood oranges."

What kind of fruit does a vampire suck on?

Neck-tarine.

GIRL: Do you know the zombie cook who moonlights as a comedian?
BOY: He has a deadpan sense of humor.

Why couldn't the monster ever count to ten?

Because 1-2-3-4-5-6-7-ATE!

How do you know when a ghost is done eating?

When all the food on his plate disappears.

What do you call a vampire who flips hamburgers?

Count Spatula.

Knock, knock.

Who's there?

Goblin.

Goblin who?

Goblin up the rest of the cookies!

What do banshees put in their coffee?

Scream and sugar.

How does an alien drink tea?

Right out of the saucer.

What did the vampire say after finishing his meal?

"Good to the last drop."

What does a cannibal order for appetizers?

Finger food.

What does a cannibal spread on his toast?

Toe jam.

Why did the cannibal eat alone?
There was no body left.

What's a cannibal's favorite cold cut?
Head cheese.

What's a cannibal's favorite instrument?
The organ.

What type of beans do cannibals like?
Kidney beans.

What did the corpse give the cannibal?
The cold shoulder.

What's the cannibal's idea of paradise?
The Garden of Eatin'.

HA HA HA HA HA HA HA HA HA HA HA HA HA

A Cannibal's Shopping List

Artichoke hearts

Hearts of palm

Cabbage head

Neck-tarines

Black-eyed peas

Ears of corn

Buns

Elbow macaroni

Fingerling potatoes

Beef cheek

Kidney beans

Liverwurst

Rump roast

Beef ribs

Leg of lamb

What penalty did the cake get called for while playing hockey?

Icing the puck.

Why did the cherry lose the car race?

It had to make a pit stop.

How do you start a food fight?

Have the pitcher hit the batter.

What did the umpire say to the pancake baseball team?

"Batter up!"

What do you call scissors that play golf?

Parsnips.

What sport does a cucumber play?

Pickleball!

What did the parrot say at the baseball game?
"Polly want a Cracker Jack."

If martial artists do karate chops, what do pigs do?
Porkchops!

Where do bakers ski?
At the Sugar Bowl resort.

Overheard on the Ski Slope

"That skier is a real hotdogger!"

Why did the umpire pour syrup on the ball?
Because it was a waffle ball.

How did the fruit salad get to first base?
It had four melon balls.

What's the softball pitcher's favorite candy?
Mounds!

What do you call pig baseball players?
Pork sliders.

How did the golfer spread his butter?

With a putter knife.

Why are doughnut makers good golfers?

Because they always get a hole in one.

MEAT MANIA

Why did the meat end up in junk mail?

It was Spam.

Why did the crockpot make a good writer?

He could cook up a meaty story.

What did the meat say when the potatoes and carrots asked for a raise?

"Let me stew on it."

What shoes do bakers wear?

Loafers.

BEEF JERKY: Give me some water!
WAITRESS: Why?
BEEF JERKY: Because I'm dehydrated!

How do you ground beef?

Take away its privileges.

Why couldn't the sausages let go of each other?

They were linked together.

What do you call a lost sausage?

The missing link.

Why did the beef brisket go to the doctor?

It had burnt ends.

Why did the ground beef go to the doctor?

It had freezer burn.

How did the shoe repairman know his grilled steak was overcooked?

It tasted like leather.

What's the shoe repairman's favorite kind of food?

Sole food.

What's the shoe repairman's least favorite food?

Tongue.

What condiment does a cowboy put on his steak?

Horseradish.

What's the best food to eat on a playground?

Sliders!

What kind of ring did the burger give the bun when he asked her to marry him?

An onion ring.

Why was the meat so rotten?

It was spoiled.

How do you lasso a cow?

With rope sausage.

Why did the vegetables break up?

Too many strains on their relationship.

What did the barbecue sauce say to the rack of beef?

"Quit ribbing me!"

What did the ribs say to the steak?

"I have a bone to pick with you."

Tell me, why is a burger made from beef called a *ham*burger?

HA HA HA HA HA HA HA HA

Which insect attacks you when you are grilling?

Mesquite-oes.

What do you get when you take a baby to a cookout?

Barbecued bibs.

What's the most honest cooked sausage?

A frank.

DANCER: What's the name of that hot dog singer?
DJ: *Frank* Sinatra.

What did Frank become after eating a hot dog?

A Frankfarter!

What's the ruler's favorite sausage?

The foot-long hot dog.

Did you hear about the hot dog that kept winning the lottery?

It was on a roll.

What kind of boots do Hungarians wear?

Goulash-es.

HA HA HA HA HA HA HA HA

How did the turkey cross the ocean?
In a gravy boat.

How did the turkey cross the country?
It rode the gravy train.

Why did the turkey pass on dessert?
It was stuffed.

Why is the turkey so lucky?
Because it has a wishbone.

What do you call a vegetarian turkey?
Tofurky.

How did the poultry farmer unlock the barn door?
With a tur-key.

How do turkeys play the drums?
With their drumsticks.

Why don't chickens follow recipes?
Because they just wing it.

How to you roast a chicken?
Make fun of it.

What did the chicken say to the gravy?

"You're smothering me."

Why wouldn't the potpie fight?

He was too chicken.

What kind of soup is afraid to be eaten?

Chicken!

What's the Disney characters' favorite game?

Donald Duck, duck, goose!

Can you say this five times fast?

"The loose goose goosed Lucy."

Why are turkeys considered rude dinner guests?

Because they gobble up their food.

Why was the pig a good joke-teller?

He was a ham!

What do pigs fly?

Pork choppers.

What do you call a Shakespearean play about pigs?

Hamlet.

What state serves the most pork bellies?

New Ham-shire!

Do chickens cook chicken fried steak?

What do you get when you tug a pig's leg?

Pulled pork.

What do you call a pig lumberjack?

A porkchop.

Knock, knock.

Who's there?

Wurst.

Wurst who?

This is the wurst knock-knock joke.

HA HA HA HA HA HA HA HA HA HA

What did the policeman say to the pancake?
"Stack 'em up!"

Knock, knock.
Who's there?
Donut.
Donut who?
Donut open the door to strangers!

What kind of bagels fly?
Plane bagels.

Which cereal do superheroes eat?
Heerios!

Knock, knock!
Who's there?
Bacon.
Bacon who?
Bacon biscuits in the oven if you want some.

HA HA HA HA HA HA HA HA

Can you say this five times fast?

"Jack stacks flapjacks on racks."

What do you get when you combine a coffee shop and a chair factory?

Coffee bean bags.

How does cereal pay the bills?

With Rice Chex.

What's the happiest breakfast cereal?

Cheerios!

How do you drink a smoothie?

With a straw-berry.

What breakfast food can't make up its mind?

A waffle.

Why did the syrup go to the doctor?

It had a cough.

HA HA HA HA HA

SYRUP TO BUTTER: What's wrong with that breakfast plate?

BUTTER: It's one pancake short of a stack.

How do you get bread to rise?

Wake it up.

How do you fix broken bread?

With glue-ten.

What dairy food do yogis eat?

Yoga-urt.

Why was the French bread invited to every party?

Because it was the toast of the town.

Knock, knock!

Who's there?

Donut.

Donut who?

Donut you know already? I have an appointment!

Why were the eccentric biscuit's parents worried?

They didn't want him to grow up to be a weird dough.

What do you get when you drop an egg?

A mess.

Sign in a Breakfast Diner

IN CASE OF FIRE, EGGS-IT HERE!

Why did the boiled egg fail the test?

It was too hard.

What do you call a Shakepearean play about eggs?

Omelet.

DINER COOK: How do you like your eggs?

EASTER BUNNY: Dyed.

How can you tell when an egg is shy?

When it doesn't want to come out of its shell.

What lane do eggs drive their cars in?

The eggspress lane!

BOY: Are you going to make breakfast?
MOM: Omelet you do it.

How does a raw egg beat a hard-boiled egg?

It out runs it.

What kind of egg grows in a garden?

Eggplant.

How do you get the devil out of deviled eggs?

With an eggsorcism!

Why was the custard getting angry?

He kept getting egged.

What's a perfect mid-meditation snack?

An *OM*-elet.

Best Self-help Books for Eggs

How to Unscramble Your Brain

How to Come Out of Your Shell

How to Tell Yokes and Crack People Up

How to Get Out of the Frying Pan

How to Build Your Nest Egg and Grow Rich!

How to Prepare an Eggs-it Plan

What do you get when a rooster lays an egg on a sidewalk?

Nothing! Roosters don't lay eggs, silly.

Knock, knock!

Who's there?

Omelet.

Omelet who?

Omelet you figure it out.

BREAD WINNERS

Can you say this five times fast?

"LuLu loves loaves."

How do you hit a meatball?

With a club sandwich.

Knock, knock!
Who's there?
Reuben.
Reuben who?
Reuben outside yet?

HA

What kind of sandwich does a skunk like?

Peanut butter and smelly.

What kind of sandwich requires a membership?

A club sandwich.

What kind of sandwich do you need to tune before you eat it?

Tunafish.

What is a liar sandwich made with?

Baloney.

BOY: I left my sandwich at home!
GIRL: Rye do you always do that?

Why was the loaf so lucky?

Because it was a bread winner.

What do you call a pig between two slices of bread?

A ham sandwich.

Why did the deli man always skip lunch?

He couldn't sandwich in any time.

HA HA HA HA HA HA HA HA

What kind of sandwiches do fishermen eat?
    Peanut butter and jellyfish!

What do you call a witch who lives in the Sahara Desert?
    A sandwitch!

What kind of bread has a bad attitude?
    Sourdough.

Why were the slices of sandwich meat shivering?
    Because they were cold cuts.

Why was the old sandwich such a bad comedian?
    Because all of its jokes were cheesy.
    (And stale!)

What do you call someone who *always* forgets his lunch?
    One sandwich short of a picnic.

How did the gardener tie a knot?

With a string bean.

What did the grandma bean say to the baby bean?

You've really sprouted!

What kind of stove works best to cook beans?

Gas.

What does a yellow bean write on?

Wax paper.

Overheard at a Barbecue

"How did Lenny find out that
Sally is sweet on him?"

"Someone spilled the beans."

What do you call a horse legume?

Pinto bean.

What kind of bean can you use for a candle?

Wax beans.

What did the worried mother say to her son when he finally got home?

"Where have you *bean*?"

What do you call a once-famous chili cook?

A has-bean.

What did the curious bean ask the military recruiter?

"Can Navy beans join the Airforce?"

HA HA HA HA HA

Which beans grow in ears?

Wax beans!

What did the car pedal say to the bean?

"Hit the gas!"

What kind of beans like to go to figurine museums?

Wax beans!

What do you get when you cross an accountant and a legume?

A bean counter.

Knock, knock.

Who's there?

Bean.

Bean who?

Bean there, done that.

HA

How did the peanut butter escape?

Its lid was ajar.

What did daddy nut say while playfully chasing baby nut?

"I'm going to cashew!"

HA HA HA HA HA HA HA HA

Who are the most musical nuts?

The Almond Brothers.

Why didn't the pecan want to go to the ballet?

Because the show was *The Nutcracker*.

What happened when the nuts and the dried fruit came to a fork in a trail?

They got trail-mixed up!

What kind of shoes does Mr. Peanut wear?

Cashews.

PEANUTS: Dare us to jump into that roaster?

ALMOND: What are you, nuts?

What kind of nut can you hang pictures on?

A walnut!

What color eyes does a nut have?

Hazel.

Knock, knock.

Who's there?

Nut.

Nut who?

Nutella you!

What kind of nut can you store socks in?
A chestnut!

JUNK FOOD FUNNIES

What's a trash collector's favorite snack?
Junk food.

Why did the pretzel get fired from his job?
He didn't cut the mustard.

What are French fries called in the United States?
French fries.

Why did the mom iron the French fries?
Because they were crinkle cut.

Why did the potato chip swerve?
To avoid the dip in the road.

What did the father potato say to his son?
"You're a chip off the old block."

HA HA HA

What do you call a bag of potato chips that hits a pothole?

Chip 'n' Dip.

What did one pretzel say to the other pretzel at the dance?

"Let's do the twist!"

Why was the pretzel so laid back?

It took everything with a grain of salt.

What party game do pretzels play?

Twister.

What do lazy kids eat while watching television?

Couch potato chips.

What do farmers in Idaho play poker with?

Potato chips.

When do potatoes get serious?

When the chips are down.

HA HA HA HA HA HA

What do you call a pretzel that works out?

A sweat-zel.

Can you say this five times fast?

"Trudie took three Twinkie treats."

Why does licorice like to read mysteries?

Because it has a lot of twists.

Why was the candy so skinny?

It was a thin mint.

Why were the candy canes rich?

They knew how to mint money.

What kind of candy grows in a garden?

Red Vines.

What kind of candy loves playgrounds?

Recess peanut butter cups!

What do you call an out-of-shape jelly bean?

A Jelly Belly.

Why did the Lifesaver and the gum get married?

They were mint to be!

What did Santa use to help him walk when he sprained his ankle?

A candy cane.

What kind of music do suckers like?

Lolli-pop!

What's the candymaker's favorite sidewalk game?

Hop butterscotch.

What do you call a chocolate lover?

A cocoa-nut!

What do you get when you cross a lightning bug and a candy bar?

Glow-in-the-dark chocolate.

Where does cocoa go on vacation?

To the Carib-bean.

What do you call a fussy violin?

Fiddle-faddle.

HA HA HA HA HA HA HA HA

Why couldn't the popcorn army make any decisions?

It had too many kernels.

What kind of dessert orbits the Earth?

Moon pies!

Which gum has killer flavor?

Spearmint.

What is chocolate's favorite hair product?

Mousse.

What did the graham cracker say to the éclair?

"You're pudding me on!"

What comes after Jell-O?

Jell-P.

What does the shoe repairman serve for dessert?

Cobbler.

What happens when you put Alaska in the oven?

You get baked Alaska!

HA HA HA HA HA

What was the sundae weather report?
Cloudy with a chance of sprinkles.

What's Cinderella's favorite pie?
Pumpkin!

Why do pies hate going to the dentist?
They don't want any more fillings.

Why did the cookie go to the doctor?
Because it was feeling a little crumby.

Overheard at a Bakery

"Did you hear that Tommy's mom
invented a new drone?"

"That's a pie-in-the-sky idea."

What do math teachers serve after dinner?
Pi.

HA HA HA

BAKED GOODIES

What do you get when you cross a groomsman and a slice of baked bread?

A wedding toast.

Why can't the baker tell the truth?

He sugarcoats everything!

What did the French baker say to his girlfriend?

"Give me a quiche."

How do you make a cinnamon roll?

Push it down a hill.

How do you butter up a roll?

Talk nicely to it.

Knock, knock.

Who's there?

Yeast.

Yeast who?

Yeast you could do is open up the door!

HA HA HA HA HA HA HA HA

Why was the bread dough so clingy?

It was knead-y.

What kind of ring did the Starbuck's barista get from her boyfriend?

A coffee ring.

Can you say this five times fast?

"Please pass the last pastry."

Where does the gingerbread man sleep at night?

On a cookie sheet.

Why couldn't the boy get out of the chair?

Because he had sticky buns.

How do you make bread rise?

Set off the alarm clock.

What type of bread is a natural gymnast?

The roll.

HA HA HA HA HA

What do cookie bakers sing at Christmastime?
"Dashing through the dough!"

Why did the first grader eat his homework?
The teacher told him it was a piece of cake.

How do you butter up a croissant?
Speak French to it.

What do you call a cake that wears a shirt, sweater, and jacket?
A layer cake.

What do you get when you flip over a cake?
An upside-down cake.

What kind of cake do you eat with a pitchfork?
Devil's food cake.

Why did the girl sleep on the cake?
Because it was a sheet cake.

Why was the baker caught stealing?
Because he really takes the cake.

HA HA HA HA HA

"Atkin ate eight cakes. Now his stomach aches!"

How does the baker make up his bed?

With cookie sheets.

What kind of points did the young baker try to earn from the head pastry chef?

Brownie points.

What kind of cake was the queen served on her birthday?

Red velvet cake with royal icing.

How does a baker sign her letters?

With hugs and quiches.

Why couldn't the baker make foot-long hot dog buns?

He only had shortbread.

HA HA HA

What did one spice say to the other when it showed up late?

"It's about thyme!"

Can you say this five times fast?

"Brother boasted 'bout his bitter butter batter."

Who discovered radioactive spice?

Marie Curry.

Why was the chef late serving dinner?

He was out of thyme.

What did the spice say when he was playing pool?

"Rack 'em up!"

HA HA HA HA HA
HA HA HA HA HA

Knock, knock.
> Who's there?

Barbie.
> Barbie who?

Barbie Q sauce!

BOY: Have you heard the joke about the butter?
GIRL: No.
BOY: It must not have spread.

What mustard makes you go to the bathroom?
> Grey Poop-on!

Why was the mustard always the last to finish the race?
> Because it wasn't able to ketchup.

How do you make jelly roll?
> Push it down a slope.

THIRST QUENCHERS

What did the Englishwoman say to the Englishman?

"You're not my cup of tea."

What did the down-and-out coffee say to the coffee pot?

"Oh, pour me."

What's black and white and red all over?

A panda swimming in strawberry Kool-Aid.

What do boxers drink?

Punch.

What does the little soda can call the big soda can?

Pop.

In what state can you find tiny bottles of pop?

Mini-soda!

Which state has the most drinking straws?

Missis-sippy.

What do you get when you milk a goat?

Kicked!

What drink can you also wear?

A tea-shirt!

What did the skim milk say to the heavy cream?

"Lighten up!"

What do you get when you mix coffee and tea?

Toffee.

How did the volleyball player serve the punch?

She spiked it!

Why did the juice fail the science test?

It couldn't concentrate.

What's the pool cleaner's favorite kind of milk?

Skim.

HA HA HA

What did the boxer say to the other boxer at the wedding reception?

I'll beat you to the punch!

Why did the gardener wash her food down with a water hose?

Because it was mouth-watering.

What did the lawyer accuse the bottled water deliverer of?

Watering down the facts.

Why should you never sue a dairy farmer?

He'll milk you for all you're worth.

A POTLUCK OF PUNS

BOY: This food tastes funny.
GIRL: Let me have a bite so I can have a good laugh.

HA HA HA HA HA HA

Best Self-help Books for Chefs

Out of the Frying Pan, into the Fire
No Reservations
Five Courses to Becoming a Better Chef
How to Sous Your Chef

What do you get when you cross a musician with rotting food?

A composter.

If you mix gum, meat chunks, and cheese sauce, what would you get?

A chewy, stewy, gooey mess!

What job did the elf get at the restaurant?

A short order cook.

What do you call absent-minded Hawaiians?

Coconut flakes.

How do you spell *boiling* with three letters?

H-O-T.

HA HA HA HA HA HA HA HA

What did the mama train say to the baby train?

"Remember to choo-choo your food before you swallow."

Where does a grocer keep his money?

In a food bank.

What will a vegan never do?

Meat you for dinner.

FARMER: Here's a glass of cow's milk.

BOY: I don't drink cow's milk.

FARMER: What do you drink?

BOY: Almond milk.

FARMER: How do you milk an almond?

What's the opposite of leftovers?

Rightunders.

What did the scientist get when he crossed a chromosome with mint leaves?

An X-spearmint.

What kind of chain can't be locked?

A food chain!

HA HA HA HA HA HA HA HA

POLITICIAN: What did you put in this soup? It's so delicious, it's criminal!

SPY: A secret ingredient.

How do you wheel groceries to the checkout?

À la cart.

BOY: Why are you eating all those foods?

GIRL: They are good for my brain.

BOY: Food for thought.

CUSTOMER: Is this gluten-free?

WAITRESS: No. Everything on the menu has a price.

Things that are Free at the Grocery Store

Gluten-free

Dairy-free

Nut-free

Sugar-free

Wheat-free

HA HA HA HA HA HA HA HA

What do you call a crazy cooker?

A crack pot!

What did the dictionary say to the encyclopedia when it lost a bet?

"Eat your words!"

What do you do when you're hungry and in a hurry?

Use feed dial.

Why did the crockpot take so long to make dinner?

It was a slow cooker.

What kind of sugar do you sprinkle in diapers?

Baby powdered sugar.

Knock, knock.

Who's there?

Anita.

Anita who?

Anita 'nother cup of sugar.

HA

How does a plumber like his food?

Piping hot!

HA HA HA HA HA HA HA HA

What kind of baths do dairymen take?
   Milk baths!

What's a trash collector's favorite stew?
   Dumpling.

What should you eat on leap-year day?
   Frog legs.

What did the mama food and daddy food have?
   Baby food.

What did the mama cream say to the baby cream when it misbehaved?
   "You're going to get a whipping!"

What ingredient do you use if you hurt your foot?
   Sugar cane.

What did the soup say when her sibling came home?
   "Hey, broth-er!"

What do bookworms eat?
   Dirty words.

HA HA HA HA HA HA HA HA

GIRL: Can circles eat square meals?

BOY: Hmm. Let me chew on that.

What are busy parents best at making for dinner?

Reservations!

SWEET & SOUR

Knock, knock!

Who's there?

Orange.

Orange who?

Orange you happy to see me?

HA

Why did the director cast the apple as the bad guy?

He was a seedy character.

Why was the apple put in jail?

It was rotten to the core.

Why was the apple so sour?

It was a crab apple.

HA HA HA HA HA

Knock, knock.

Who's there?

Cider.

Cider who?

Be cider, who else lives here?

Did you hear that the McIntosh and Golden Delicious got married?

Yes, I hope they live apple-y ever after.

If an apple a day keeps the doctor away, who does a head of garlic keep away?

Everyone!

Why did the apple work out?

To strengthen its core.

Can you say this five times fast?

"Spiders sip cider beside her."

Why was Adam in love with Eve?

She was the apple of his eye.

HA HA HA HA HA HA HA HA

What's an old lady's favorite apple?

Granny Smith.

What do you call an apple that gets stuck in a man's throat?

Adam!

What did the apple say to the larva?

"You can't worm your way out of this."

Orange door hinge.

Who says orange doesn't rhyme with anything?

How do you make an orange?

Mix red and yellow.

What kind of books do oranges read?

Pulp fiction.

How did the orange lose the fight?

He was beaten to a pulp.

HA HA HA

Why do oranges have good eyesight?
They contain vitamin "see."

How do you make a lemonade stand?
Pull away its chair.

What did the lemon say when he wanted a kiss?
"Pucker up!"

Knock, knock!
Who's there?
Orange.
Orange who?
Orange you late for school?

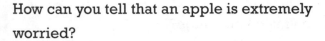

How can you tell that an apple is extremely worried?
She's be-cider self.

How did the lemon get through the tiny door?
It squeezed through.

What is a lemon's favorite type of bread?
Sourdough.

HA HA HA

Best Self-help Books for Lemons

How to Get Your Friends Back When Things Go Sour
How to Squeeze Extra Money from a Small Allowance
How to Make Lemonade . . . from Lemons!
When Life Gives You Lemons, Say Thank You!
Suck It Up!
Pucker Power!
Squeeze the Most Out of Life
Money Doesn't Grow on Trees, but You Can!

What did the grandma lemon say to her grandchild?

"Give me a squeeze!"

What do you call a cat that eats lemons?

A sour puss.

Why did everyone in the fridge avoid the lemon?

He was in a sour mood.

Knock, knock.

Who's there?

Orange.

Orange who?

Orange you glad I didn't tell another joke?

Natasha Wing loves a good pun and appreciates how language offers so many ways to twist and turn words. Even as a kid, Natasha enjoyed scrambling up words to make people laugh.

Natasha is best known for her paperback series based on the popular poem *The Night Before Christmas.* Her titles include *The Night Before Easter* —the original book in the series—and *The Night Before Kindergarten*, which has sold more than two million copies and has regularly appeared on bestseller lists since its publication in 2001. Her other picture books include *Bagel In Love*, which *Booklist* called "humorous, lighthearted fare with a heartening ending and chuckle-worthy jokes"; *Jalapeño Bagels,* now in its twenty-third printing; and *An Eye for Color: The Story of Josef Albers*, which was an ALA Notable, a Junior Library Guild Selection, a California Reading Association's Eureka! Honor Book, and a 2012 Grand Canyon Reader nominee. Natasha lives in Fort Collins, Colorado, with her husband, Dan, and cat, Purrsia. Learn more about Natasha at natashawing.com.